W0008988

A CHRISTMAS CAROL

by Alan Harris

based on the story by Charles Dickens

⫴SAMUEL FRENCH⫴

samuelfrench.co.uk

MUSIC USE NOTE

Licensees are solely responsible for obtaining formal written permission from copyright owners to use copyrighted music in the performance of this play and are strongly cautioned to do so. If no such permission is obtained by the licensee, then the licensee must use only original music that the licensee owns and controls. Licensees are solely responsible and liable for all music clearances and shall indemnify the copyright owners of the play(s) and their licensing agent, Samuel French, against any costs, expenses, losses and liabilities arising from the use of music by licensees. Please contact the appropriate music licensing authority in your territory for the rights to any incidental music.

USE OF COPYRIGHT MUSIC

A licence issued by Samuel French Ltd to perform this play does not include permission to use the incidental music specified in this copy. Where the place of performance is already licensed by the PERFORMING RIGHT SOCIETY (PRS) a return of the music used must be made to them. If the place of performance is not so licensed then application should be made to the PRS, 2 Pancras Square, London, N1C 4AG (www.prsformusic.com). A separate and additional licence from PHONOGRAPHIC PERFORMANCE LTD, 1 Upper James Street, London W1F 9DE (www.ppluk.com) is needed whenever commercial recordings are used.

IMPORTANT BILLING AND CREDIT REQUIREMENTS

If you have obtained performance rights to this title, please refer to your licensing agreement for important billing and credit requirements.

ABOUT THE ADAPTER

Alan Harris has written plays for theatres throughout the UK and internationally, including Paines Plough, Manchester Royal Exchange, the Sherman Theatre and National Theatre Wales. He won a Judges Award at the Bruntwood Prize for *How My Light Is Spent*.

Shows at the Edinburgh Fringe have included *Love, Lies and Taxidermy* (Theatr Clwyd/Paines Plough), *For All I Care* (National Theatre Wales) and *Sugar Baby* (Dirty Protest). He wrote the book for *A Scythe of Time* at the New York Musical Theatre Festival.

The Left Behind was recently broadcast by BBC Three (a BBC Studios commission) and he's writing new dramas for Hartswood West, Bad Wolf, BBC Studios Wales and a new theatre play for Theatr Clwyd, *For The Grace Of You Go I*.

He has also written plays for BBC Radio 4 and Radio 3, and Amazon Audible.

ADAPTER'S NOTE

This production was set in Victorian Mold, North Wales, but, of course, it can be set in a different town. It was originally staged with a cast of five along with a community cast but, again, that is flexible.

A CHRISTMAS CAROL

The world première of Charles Dickens' *A Christmas Carol* adapted by Alan Harris took place at Theatr Clwyd on 13 December 2019 with the following cast:

CAST (in alphabetical order)

BOB CRATCHIT/FEZZIWIG/ RICHARD/SCHOOLMASTER	Matthew Bulgo
MS AUBIN/BELLE/ GHOST OF CHRISTMAS PRESENT/ BEGGAR	Amy Drake
SCROOGE	Steven Elliott
MRS ROBERTS/GHOST OF CHRISTMAS PAST	Kerry Peers
TINY TIM/GHOST OF CHRISTMAS FUTURE	Lewis Lowry, Dylan Roberts, Ellis Williams

COMMUNITY OF MOLD
Beth Armstrong, Sean Bates, Faye Briggs, Liz Carter-Jones, Karen Campbell, Gwyneth Dillon, Gavin Hayes, Harold Hewitt, Lady Annmaria Jones, Maisie Langridge, Jeni Lee, Rachel Quayle, Rebecca Snowdon, Stephen Taylor, William Wood, Sam Wyse.

CREATIVE TEAM

ADAPTED BY	Alan Harris
DIRECTOR	Liz Stevenson
DESIGNER	Frankie Bradshaw
COMPOSER/MUSICAL DIRECTOR	Barnaby Race
LIGHTING DESIGNER	Matt Leventhall
SOUND DESIGNER	Alexandra Faye Braithwaite
MOVEMENT DIRECTOR	Sian Williams
CASTING DIRECTOR	Peter Hunt CDG
ASSISTANT DIRECTOR Theatr Clwyd Carne Traineeship	Francesca Goodridge
COMPANY STAGE MANAGER	Sarah Thomas
DEPUTY STAGE MANAGER	Caroline Sheard
PRODUCER	Tom Bevan
COMMUNITY PRODUCER	Alice Evans
PRODUCTION MANAGER	Jim Davis
COSTUME SUPERVISOR	Flora Moyes

CAST

MATTHEW BULGO | BOB CRATCHIT/ FEZZIWIG/RICHARD/SCHOOLMASTER

Matthew trained at LAMDA.
His theatre credits include: *The Cherry Orchard, The Sleeping Beauties, Clytemnestra, A Christmas Caro*l (Sherman Theatre); *All My Sons* (Theatr Clwyd); *Lord of the Flies* (Sherman Theatre/ Theatr Clwyd); *The Insatiable, Inflatable Candylion, Praxis Makes Perfect* (National Theatre Wales); *I'm With The Band, Horizontal Collaboration* (Traverse Theatre); *Kenny Morgan* (Arcola); *Under Milk Wood* (Royal and Derngate); *The Prince Hamlet* (Toronto Dance Theatre); *Play, Silence* (The Other Room); *Blue/ Orange* (Canoe Theatre); *The City* (Living Pictures); *Adventures in the Skin Trade* (Theatr Iolo); *Much Ado About Nothing, A Midsummer Night's Dream* (Mappa Mundi); *Breakfast Hearts, Choirplay, Patching Havoc* (Theatre 503); *Feeding Time, The Play About The Baby* (BAC); *Hamlet* (Middle Temple Hall).
Matthew is an Associate Director of Dirty Protest Theatre and also works as a playwright and dramaturg.

AMY DRAKE | MS AUBIN/BELLE/ GHOST OF CHRISTMAS PRESENT/ BEGGAR

Amy graduated from ALRA North in 2013 and has since appeared in *Emmerdale, Hollyoaks* and *Cold Feet*. Commercials include *Lidl, Ladbrokes* and a Christmas campaign for *Tesco* in 2018. Theatre credits include; *We're Going On A Bear Hunt* (Bolton Octagon); *Treasure Island*

(The Dukes Lancaster); *My Mother Said I Never Should* (Theatre By the Lake); *Under the Market Roof* (Junction 8 Theatre); *Babushka* (Hard Graft Theatre) and *Tinned Up* (Oldham Coliseum).

STEVEN ELLIOTT | SCROOGE

Theatre includes: *Frankenstein, The Winter's Tale* (Royal National Theatre); *Titus Andronicus, Julius Caesar, Revenger's Tragedy, Henry V, Twelfth Night, Pentecost, The Bite of the Night, The Jew of Malta, Measure for Measure, The Merry Wives of Windsor, A Christmas Carol, Words, Words, Words* (Royal Shakespeare Company); *The LadyKillers* (UK Tour), *The Devil Inside Him* (National Theatre Wales); *Dancing at Lughnasa* (Abbey, Dublin); *King Lear* (Almeida, London); *True West* (Glasgow Citz); *Inherit the Wind, Dumb Show* (New Vic, Stoke); *Arcadia* (Bristol Old Vic); *The Winter's Tale, The Weir* (Sherman, Cardiff); Associate Artist at Theatr Clwyd – Scrooge in *A Christmas Carol, Macbeth, A Chorus of Disapproval, Arcadia, Troilus and Cressida, Measure for Measure, The Suicide, Noises Off, Jumpy, Cyrano de Bergerac.*
Television includes: *The Crown, Da Vinci's Demons, Judge John Deed, Porthpenwaig, Inspector Morse, Holby City, Harpur and Isles, Van der Valk, Art that Shook the World, 90 Days in Hollywood, Ghostboat, Rhinoceros, Mike Bassett, Manager.*
Film includes: *Hamlet, Les Miserables, Cold Earth, Rise of the Appliances, Green Monkey, Trauma, Time Bandits*, digital recording of *True West* and *Frankenstein* (NT Live).
Website: stevenelliott.org

KERRY PEERS | MRS ROBERTS/GHOST OF CHRISTMAS PAST

Wave Me Goodbye, Much Ado About Nothing, Jumpy, A Streetcar Named Desire, One Flew Over the Cuckoo's Nest (Theatr Clwyd).

Other theatre credits include: *The Words are Coming Now* (Theatre503); *Pride and Prejudice* (Nottingham Playhouse/York Theatre Royal); *Brighton Beach Memoirs* (Manchester Theatre Awards Winner); *The Father* (Manchester Theatre Awards nominee); *Dead Funny* (Manchester Theatre Awards nominee); *Absent Friends* (Oldham Coliseum & Tour); *Shirley Valentine* one-woman show (Frinton Summer Theatre); *Billy Liar* (Liverpool Playhouse); *The Diary of Anne Frank* (York Theatre Royal/Touring Consortium); *A Song at Twilight, Paradise Bound* (Liverpool Everyman); *Bloody Poetry, Les Liaisons Dangereuses* (RSC).

Her television credits include: numerous recurring characters: Dr Trish Wendell in *Clink*, Helen Carey in *Brookside* (Mersey TV) and WDC Suzi Croft in *The Bill* (Thames TV). Kerry can currently be seen playing Marion Logan in *Coronation Street*. Other television credits include: *Doctors, Casualty* (BBC), *Open Doors* (LA Productions), *Butterfly* (Red Productions), *Bulletproof* (Vertigo for Sky), *Hollyoaks, The Case* (Lime Pictures), *Shameless* (Channel 4), *The Royal Today* (ITV), *Family Affairs* (Channel 5), *September Song* (Granada TV). Kerry has also performed in many Radio plays for BBC Radio 4.

DYLAN ROBERTS | TINY TIM/GHOST OF CHRISTMAS FUTURE

Dylan is twelve and has been a part of Trap Door Theatre School for over three years, his roles have included: The Artful Dodger in *Oliver!* and The White Rabbit in *Alice in Wonderland.*

ELLIS WILLIAMS | TINY TIM/GHOST OF CHRISTMAS FUTURE

Ellis is nine and has appeared in Bill Kenwright's production of *Joseph and the Amazing Technicolor Dreamcoat* starring Union J's Jaymi Hensley. *A Christmas Carol* is Ellis' first solo appearance. Ellis is a keen rugby player, a member of Wrexham Rugby Club Under 10's he can be found on the rugby pitch every Sunday morning come rain or shine.

LEWIS LOWRY | TINY TIM/GHOST OF CHRISTMAS FUTURE

Lewis is very excited to play one of the Tiny Tims this year in his favourite theatre, having previously starred in *Peter Pan*, *Oliver!* and *Bugsy Malone* and is also looking forward to his role in *Made in Dagenham* in 2020.

CREATIVE TEAM

LIZ STEVENSON | DIRECTOR

Liz is the Artistic Director at Theatre by the Lake, Keswick. She won the 2015 JMK Young Director Award. Her production of *Barbarians* at the Young Vic was nominated for a 2016 Olivier Award for Outstanding Achievement in an Affiliate Theatre. She is the co-founder of Junction 8 Theatre.

Work as a Director: *Lancastrians, Under The Market Roof* (Junction 8 Theatre); *The Secret Garden* (York Theatre Royal, Theatre by the Lake); *Handbagged* (Theatre by the Lake); *How My Light Is Spent* (Royal Exchange Theatre, Sherman Theatre, Theatre by the Lake); *Macbeth* (Dukes Theatre, Lancaster), *Barbarians* (Young Vic).

FRANKIE BRADSHAW | DESIGNER

Frankie Bradshaw together with director Lynette Linton recently won The Stage Best Creative West End Debut Award for Sweat at the Gielgud Theatre 2019. She was a Jerwood Young Designer in 2017 and won the Off-West End Best Set Design award in 2016.

Frankie's design credits for theatre include; *Sweat* (Donmar Warehouse/West End); *Skellig* (Nottingham Playhouse); *Two Trains Running* (Royal & Derngate/ETT UK Tour); *Cinderella* (Lyric Hammersmith); *Kiss Me Kate, Jerusalem, Nesting, Robin Hood* (Watermill Theatre); *Napoli Brooklyn* (UK Tour/Park Theatre), *Trying It On* (UK Tour/RSC/Royal Court); *Cookies* (Theatre Royal Haymarket); *On The Exhale* (Traverse Theatre); *This Is* (Arts Ed); *Hansel* (Salisbury Playhouse); *Acceptance* (Hampstead Theatre); *Mercury Fur, Saved* and *Colder Than Here* (GSMD); *Easter* (RADA), *Oxy and the Morons* (New Wolsey Theatre); *Jess and Joe Forever, Di and Viv and Rose* (Stephen Joseph Theatre) and *Assata Taught Me* (Gate Theatre). For opera she has designed *Macbeth, Idomeneo* and *Elizabetta* for English Touring Opera. www.frankiebradshawdesign.com

BARNABY RACE | COMPOSER/MUSICAL DIRECTOR

Barnaby is a classically trained musician who studied as a Chorister at Canterbury Cathedral, Trinity College of Music and The Guildhall School of Music and Drama.

Musical Director and Composer credits include: *CinderELLA*

The Musical (The Nuffield Theatre); *Romeo and Juliet* (Secret Cinema); *The Secret Garden* (Theatre by the Lake/York Theatre Royal); *The Last Days of Anne Boleyn* (Historic Royal Palaces/Tower of London); *Babe, the Sheep-Pig* (Polka Theatre/UK Tour); *Pine* (Hampstead Theatre); *One Flew Over The Cuckoo Nest* (Secret Cinema); *Minotaur* (Polka Theatre/Clwyd Theatr Cymru); *The Devil Speaks True* (Goat and Monkey); *Clybourne Park*, *As You Like It* (RADA); *Dracula* (LAMDA); *How to be Immortal* (Soho Theatre/National Tour); *A Feast with the Gods* (Almeida Theatre); *Alice: The Ballet* (Marlowe Theatre Canterbury); *Cesario* (Assistant MD. National Theatre); *The Class* (NYT) and workshops for Aramco/NYT in Saudi Arabia. Barnaby was Musical Director for the Welcome Ceremonies at the Glasgow Commonwealth Games.

Film and Advert credits include: commissions for Ikea, Argos and various large campaigns for Graff Diamonds; additional music, orchestral arranging/vocal recording for *The Harry Hill Movie*; songwriting for *Lizard Girl* (BBC); composition and sound design for *Playing the Game* (IRIS Film Festival).

MATT LEVENTHALL | LIGHTING DESIGNER

Matt trained at RADA. Recent credits include: *Trial By Laughter* (Watermill and UK Tour); *No Kids* (UK, USA and Hong Kong Tour); *Turn of The Screw* (Mercury and UK Tour), *The Secret Garden* (York Theatre Royal), *Hamlet* (Kenneth Branagh Theatre Company, Associate LD); *The Terrible Infants* (Wilton's); *The Events* (Mercury Theatre); *Light* (Barbican, Bristol Old Vic and European Tour); *Barbarians* (Young Vic); *The Comedy About a Bank Robbery* (Criterion, Associate LD); *My Mother Never Said I Should* (St James Theatre, Associate LD), *The Collector* (The Vaults Theatre); *The Vaudevillans* (Assembly); *Captain Flinn and the Pirate Dinosaurs* (Pleasance and UK Tour); *Moth* (Hope Mill); *Hamlet is Dead: No Gravity* (Arcola); *Ant Street* (Arcola); *Lady Anna All At Sea* (Park Theatre); *Scarlet* (Southwark Playhouse); *Islands* (New Diorama, Underbelly); *God's Own Country* (Zoo); *Sikes and Nancy* (Trafalgar Studios and UK Tour); *Suffolk Stories* (Theatre Royal Bury St Edmunds); *Who Framed Roger Rabbit?* (Secret Cinema, Site Specific); *Fishskin Trousers* (Finborough); *Wild West End* (Pleasance); *Bed* (Lakeside Arts Nottingham); *Madame Butterfly* (Leatherhead Theatre and UK Tour);

Fresher The Musical (Pleasance); *The Songs of My Life* (Garrick Theatre); *TEDx London* (The Roundhouse). For a full list of credits visit www.mllx.co.uk

ALEXANDRA FAYE BRAITHWAITE | SOUND DESIGNER
Theatre credits include: *Light Falls* (Royal Exchange); *Groan Ups* (Vaudeville Theatre); *Enough, How Not To Drown* (The Traverse); *The Audience* (Nuffield Theatre); *Hamlet* (Leeds Playhouse); *Cougar, Dealing with Clair* (Orange Tree Theatre); *My Name Is Rachel Corrie* (The Faction, Beirut); *Things of Dry Hours* (Young Vic); *Talking Heads* (West Yorkshire Playhouse); *Toast* (The Lowry & Traverse); *Grotty* (The Bunker); *Grumpy Old Women IIII* (Uk Tour); *Acceptance* (Hampstead Theatre); *Chicken Soup* (Sheffield Crucible); *Dublin Carol* (Sherman Theatre); *Kanye the First* (Hightide); *Room* (Theatre Royal Stratford East & The Abbey); *If I Was Queen* (The Almeida); *Rudolph* (West Yorkshire Playhouse); *The Remains of Maisie Duggan* (The Abbey); *The Tempest* (The Royal & Derngate); *Simon Slack* (Soho Theatre); *Diary of a Madman* (The Gate & Traverse); *The Rolling Stone* (The Orange Tree), *Happy To Help* (Park Theatre); *The Future* (The Yard); *My Beautiful Black Dog* (Southbank Centre); *Hamlet Is Dead, No Gravity* (The Arcola); *Juicy & Delicious* (Nuffield Theatre); *Remote* (Theatre Royal Plymouth); *The Shelter* (Riverside Studios); *Lonely Soldiers* (Arts Theatre).

SIÂN WILLIAMS | MOVEMENT DIRECTOR
Siân Williams co-founded The Kosh physical theatre company in 1982.
Credits range from Shakespeare's Globe to Broadway, Edinburgh to Glastonbury.
Productions include artist Kate Bush's *Before The Dawn* concerts; *Wolf Hall* (BBC 2, adapted from Hilary Mantel's novel); *Richard III* (Belasco Theatre Broadway); *Henry IV part 1&2, Henry V, As You Like It* (Shakespeare's Globe); *A Midsummer Night's Dream, Troilus* and *Cressida* (RSC); James Graham's political drama *Labour of Love* in the West End; *Beauty and the Beast, The Secret Garden* (Theatre By The Lake); *My People* (Theatr Clwyd/Invertigo).
Most recently choreographed and currently performing in Gluck's opera *Orfeo Ed Eurydice* for Purefeo Productions.

PETER HUNT CDG | CASTING DIRECTOR

Peter started out as an actor before moving across to the world of Production and Casting. Now splitting his time between London and Manchester Peter and his team work on a diverse range of projects spanning the worlds of Theatre, Film, TV, Radio, Music Videos and TV Commercials.

Recent Screen Projects include: *Hollyoaks* (Channel 4); *Thick as Thieves* and *Aiysha* (both for Steel Films). *To Know Him* (Pencil Trick Productions).

Recent Theatre Projects include: *Lancastrians* & *Under the Market Roof* (both for Junction 8 Theatre).

In 2018 Peter was voted as Casting Director of the Year and his 2019 projects have already received various award nominations to include the NTA's and BAFTA. Peter is currently working on a new International TV Drama project due for release in 2020.

FRANCESCA GOODRIDGE | ASSISTANT DIRECTOR

(Theatr Clwyd Carne Traineeship)

Francesca trained at Liverpool Institute for Performing Arts (LIPA) achieving a BA Hons in Acting. She is now one of the two directors of Theatr Clwyd's Carne Traineeship for Directors in Wales. Francesca has experience as an actor, vocalist, choreographer and director. She is the former Trainee Director of The Other Room Theatre in Cardiff.

Theatr Clwyd

THE AWARD-WINNING THEATR CLWYD IS WALES' BIGGEST PRODUCING THEATRE.

Based in Flintshire, the gateway to North Wales, since 1976 Theatr Clwyd has been a cultural powerhouse producing world-class theatre, from the UK Theatre Award-winning musical *The Assassination Of Katie Hopkins* and Olivier award-winning West End comedy *Home, I'm Darling* in co-production with the National Theatre, to the site specific, immersive *The Great Gatsby*, the epic community show *Mold Riots* and its sell-out rock 'n' roll pantomimes. Led by Artistic Director Tamara Harvey and Executive Director Liam Evans-Ford, Theatr Clwyd's world-class team of workshop, wardrobe and scenic artists, props makers and technicians ensure the skills vital to a vibrant theatre industry are nurtured right in the heart of Wales. Alongside the three theatre spaces, cinema, café, bar and art galleries, Theatr Clwyd works with the community in many different guises across all art forms and is recognised as a cultural leader for its cross-generational theatre groups, work in youth justice and diverse programme of arts, health and wellbeing.

Find out more: www.theatrclwyd.com
Twitter: @ClwydTweets
Follow Us: Facebook.com/TheatrClwyd

CHARACTERS

EBENEZER SCROOGE – (45–65)
A miserly man deeply affected by his own father's spiral into debt. The losses he's suffered in life have given him a hard shell. Has run a money-lending business alone (apart from his clerk Bob Cratchit) since the death of his partner, Marley. It's not that Scrooge dislikes Christmas, he finds it all a bit obscene. Sees himself as a realist. Also thinks he's funnier than people find him. Has it in his heart, of course, to transform from the most miserly to the most generous of men.

BOB CRATCHIT / SCHOOLMASTER / FEZZIWIG / RICHARD (30–40)
Each of these characters has a kind heart – Bob, especially, wears his heart on his sleeve.

BEGGAR / MS AUBIN / BELLE / GHOST OF CHRISTMAS PRESENT (20–30)
There's a hope and strength about these characters. A mixture of optimism and pragmatism.

MRS ROBERTS / GHOST OF CHRISTMAS PAST (30–60)
Both are sarcastic, they've seen the world and its problems and know what a struggle life can be. Mrs Roberts loves to talk. Both have a bit of a sharp tongue.

TINY TIM / YOUNG SCROOGE / GHOST OF CHRISTMAS FUTURE
There is an innocence to these characters – but also a wit and naughty side (especially Tiny Tim). They feel the importance of family (whatever that means – blood relative or not, it's about connecting to other people; they need that to survive).

TOWNSPEOPLE / TRADESPEOPLE / DICK / MRS SAUNDERS / CHURCH CHRISTMAS SHOW CAST / MRS TOPPER / PARTY-GOERS

In this production Marley is never seen – his voice is heard and his presence felt through lighting and sound design.

Thanks to:
Gerrards Bakery, Mold,
Spavens, Mold,
Holywell Library,
Mold Library
Phylip Harries

CHARACTER LIST

EBENEZER SCROOGE

BOB CRATCHIT

BEGGAR

MRS ROBERTS

TINY TIM

MS AUBIN

MARLEY

GHOST OF CHRISTMAS PAST

YOUNG SCROOGE

SCHOOLMASTER

FEZZIWIG

DICK

MRS SAUNDERS

BELLE

GHOST OF CHRISTMAS PRESENT

GHOST OF CHRISTMAS FUTURE

MRS TOPPER

MR TOPPER

RICHARD

The year is 1843. High Street, Mold. Christmas Eve. The bells of St Mary's Church ring out. There's a hustle and bustle about the street, which is a little threadbare at the edges – the town is doing its best to get into the spirit of Christmas but there's an obvious lack of cash around. There are stalls, street vendors and shops selling Christmassy things (including sweets, mistletoe and turkey). It's fun and a bit anarchic. There is only one building not decorated – **SCROOGE**'s *office.*

As the audience enters they are each given three tokens to spend in the street. Some things must be too expensive for one person to buy – they will have to club together. There is one thing that is worth more than all the tokens in the High Street – the Big Prize Turkey.

In the street there are carol singers and a tree where children (and adults) can write down what they think is the most special thing about Christmas and hang their messages on the branches. (Maybe these are on snowflakes made of card?)

EBENEZER SCROOGE *is collecting money on debts owed by the shopkeepers / the shoppers / the audience.* **BOB CRATCHIT** *accompanies him and (apologetically) records every payment in a notebook.* **BOB** *keeps getting distracted by talking to people (asking how their family is, etc.).*

Despite **SCROOGE** *putting a downer on things, the townspeople break into singing carols.* **BOB** *loves it. It's too much for* **SCROOGE** *– he retreats towards his office. Above the door it says:* **MARLEY** *and* **SCROOGE**, *Money Lenders, est. 1826.*

BOB *is exchanging pleasantries with people when:*

SCROOGE Bob Cratchit! I'm not paying you fifteen shillings a week to gossip.

BOB Yes, Mr Scrooge.

A **BEGGAR** *grabs hold of* **SCROOGE***'s coat tails.*

BEGGAR Please, sir, can you spare a farthing for a cup of cheer?

SCROOGE You must be new in town.

BEGGAR Yes sir, arrived this morning. Mold's a lovely town. But cold. I'm living in an old army tent behind the/church.

> **SCROOGE** *tries to remove the* **BEGGAR***'s hand. As he's trying,* **MRS ROBERTS,** *who is selling sprigs of mistletoe, holds a sprig above* **SCROOGE***'s head and gives him "pretend" kisses. When he turns she's far too close.*

MRS ROBERTS Oh, Mr Scrooge, can I have a quick word?

SCROOGE You've never been quick, Mrs Roberts.

MRS ROBERTS Can you believe our roof has fallen in? Mr Roberts is at this very moment standing, like this, in our bedroom, dressed only in his undergarments, holding it up. If it rains, well, I shudder to think – we have to get it fixed, you can see that? And we were wondering, the three pounds we owe you, I don't think we're going to be able to, what with Mr Roberts holding up the roof, like this, pay you this week and this is a special circumstance and me and Mr Cratchit being neighbours and /

SCROOGE Cratchit?

BOB Yes sir?

SCROOGE When is Mrs Roberts's next payment due?

As **BOB** *flicks through the book:*

BOB Mrs Roberts... Mrs Roberts...

MRS ROBERTS It's Christmas Day, this is very good of you Mr Scrooge, thank /

SCROOGE Tomorrow it is then, or I send in the bailiffs. Cratchit!

He enters his office, giving **MRS ROBERTS** *and the* **BEGGAR** *no hope.*

BOB I'm sorry Mrs Roberts, I'll see if I can work on him. *(giving the* **BEGGAR** *a coin)* Here you go.

MRS ROBERTS You'd sooner fashion a slab of granite with your fingers. *(beat)* Sorry Bob, I know it's not your fault.

BOB But I work for him, doing his bidding – doesn't that make me even worse in a way?

MRS ROBERTS I know you only do it for Tiny Tim.

BOB Where is Tim? Thought he was with you today?

MRS ROBERTS He's rehearsing.

BOB Rehearsing? Mrs Roberts?

MRS ROBERTS A Christmas surprise for you. He wants to be in the Christmas church show but I don't think he's strong enough – last night, through the walls, I heard him coughing.

BOB He's not getting any better.

MRS ROBERTS He so wants to be in the performance so I said he can learn a song and sing it next year. He's practising now – he's going to sing it for you on Christmas Day. Act surprised when he does.

BOB *acts surprised.*

Maybe you could do with some rehearsals yourself.

BOB I'm going to ask Mr Scrooge for an hour off this afternoon – take Tiny Tim to the doctor.

MRS ROBERTS Good luck with that.

SCROOGE Don't test me Cratchit!

BOB *acts surprised.*

MRS ROBERTS Better.

BOB Good luck with the roof Mrs Roberts. *(with a wink)* And with the rehearsing...

BOB *runs to the office.*

MRS ROBERTS *joins* **TINY TIM** *at Mrs Foggarty's (one of the shops).*

MRS ROBERTS Now Tim, you found a song you want to sing?

TINY TIM That boy there *(one of the audience)* taught me one.

MRS ROBERTS *(to the audience member)* That's kind of you.

TINY TIM *starts to hum the tune to* ***"SILENT NIGHT"*** */ warms up.*

Oh I like this one.

TINY TIM *starts to sing:*

TINY TIM
SILENT FART, STINKY FART
POLLUTES THE AIR WHEN MY CHEEKS PART
ROUND YON TOWN ALL WAS PEACEFUL AND CALM
THEN I WENT AND DROPPED MY BOMB
AND I THINK EVERYONE KNOWS IT WAS MEEEEEE
I SHOULDN'T HAVE HAD THOSE BEANS FOR TEA

SILENT FART /

MRS ROBERTS That's enough! *(to the audience member)* You should be ashamed of yourself. Pure muck! You'll have to think of something else!

In his office, **SCROOGE** *lights a single candle to work by and gives a lump of coal to* **BOB**.

BOB A lump of coal? What am I supposed to do with that?

SCROOGE Huddle close to it to keep warm. *(pause)* If you get really cold, light it.

BOB Mr Scrooge?

SCROOGE *goes about his work.*

I was wondering, you know I have a little boy, Tiny Tim, well it's vital I get him to the doctor's before /

SCROOGE Suppose you'll want all day off tomorrow? It being Christmas Day.

BOB If it's convenient.

SCROOGE It's not – and it's not fair. If I was to stop half-crown for it you'd think yourself hard done by, I'm sure. Yet – you don't think me hard done by when I pay a day's wages for no work, do you?

BOB About my boy, he's not very well and I was wondering this afternoon if, it being Christmas Eve /

MS AUBIN *bustles into the office. She's blowing bubbles from a small bubble bottle.*

MS AUBIN *(heavy French accent)* Enchanté, Monsieur Marley I presume?

SCROOGE Marley is dead – he died seven years ago this very night.

MS AUBIN Marley is mort?

BOB Oh yeah, he's dead. Marley is definitely dead. Dead as a door nail. Dead. Dead as a door knocker. Dead as a dodo. Deader than the dead of the night. Dead as /

SCROOGE Thank you Cratchit, I think we've established Marley is definitely dead.

MS AUBIN Then you'll be Monsieur Scrooge.

SCROOGE We've a sharp one on our hands here, Cratchit.

MS AUBIN As this is the festive season, I can't believe it's Christmas Eve already, where does the time / go?

SCROOGE Time is money.

MS AUBIN I'm collecting for the poor in the parish of Mold. I'm thinking of setting up a central point in the church to hand out basic foodstuffs and clothes and whatzenots and what with the rising cost of living, the lack of well-paid jobs, it's an austere time for the best of us I'm sure you'll agree /

SCROOGE Where's the profit in that?

MS AUBIN Oh, no, we're not going to make a profit /

BOB Are you French?

MS AUBIN Whatever gave it away? *(to* **SCROOGE***)* But you don't get nuffin for your cash, mon cheri – you get one of these! It's a bubble machine! I'm sure a fine gentleman like yourself would like to contribute...?

BOB Oh dear *(He knows what's coming...)*

Behind **SCROOGE***'s back he tries to signal to* **MS AUBIN** *that she should drop the subject...*

SCROOGE Are there no prisons?

MS AUBIN Plenty.

SCROOGE And the workhouses? The Poorhouse? Still in operation?

MS AUBIN *Oui, regretment,* they are.

SCROOGE Glad to hear it.

MS AUBIN Hmmm. What shall I put you down for? Your contribution?

SCROOGE Nothing.

MS AUBIN You want to stay anonymous, I totally understand, I too am the shy / sort.

SCROOGE I wish to be left alone. I don't make merry myself at Christmas and I can't afford to make idle people merry. Charity is not my business. I pay taxes to help pay for the establishments I've mentioned. Those who are badly off – it's their own fault they're poor. They can go to the workhouse.

MS AUBIN Many would rather die than let their families /

SCROOGE If they would rather die, they'd better get on with it – and decrease the surplus population.

MS AUBIN *(heavy Welsh accent)* Look, butty, you going to give any cash to the poor or not? There's people proper starving out there.

SCROOGE No. Good day to you, madam – and take your blasted bubbles with you!

SCROOGE *bustles* **MS AUBIN** *out of the office.*

I knew she wasn't French.

As she leaves, **MS AUBIN** *recovers her French persona and speaks to the audience as she walks away.*

MS AUBIN Why are some people so mean? I'm only wanting to spread some Christmas joy, mai oui? After all it's Christmas Eve – a time of magic."

SCROOGE *turns to* **BOB**.

SCROOGE Something you wanted to ask me Cratchit?

BOB No, I see now that it's pointless.

SCROOGE How much do the people of Mold owe me Cratchit?

BOB Uh, off hand, not sure /

SCROOGE About time we had a reckoning – write me a list of all debts and add it up. A man should know his worth.

BOB *picks up three volumes of ledgers.*

BOB You want me to count up all these debts? There's tons of them.

SCROOGE I find that a comfort.

BOB I'll be doing sums till New Year.

SCROOGE You'd better get on with it then!

BOB really wants to say something – but knows he shouldn't. He starts work.

The carols continue outside and drift away.

Time passes.

The crowd in the street starts to thin as the weak sun goes down.

The clock strikes six o'clock. **BOB** *takes this as a sign that the working day has ended and gets up.*

That's the quickest you've moved all day.

BOB It is Christmas Eve sir.

SCROOGE As everyone seems keen to remind me.

BOB I can go home? I've probably missed the doctor now... And tomorrow...sir? Christmas Day...sir?

SCROOGE Be here extra early on Boxing Day, yes?

BOB Of course. Thank you.

> **BOB** *gathers his belongings.*

Mr Scrooge? Where are you spending Christmas Day?

SCROOGE Thought you wanted to go home?

BOB If you're on your own sir, you're very welcome to spend it with me and Tiny Tim... we've a small goose.

SCROOGE Oh I get it – you want me to lavish you with presents and pay for a meal, that it?

BOB No, sir, I /

SCROOGE I know your game Bob Cratchit.

Frustrated, **BOB***, starts to leave.*

Before he does, he puts a small, wrapped present on **SCROOGE***'s desk and backs away.*

BOB Merry Christmas.

SCROOGE What the...?

BOB I did think about suggesting a Secret Santa but with only two of us in the office... this is just a small something. Tiny Tim made it. Merry Christmas.

SCROOGE Humbug! What's merry about it? What's good about it?

BOB I said my Tim made it – doesn't that mean anything to / you?

SCROOGE What right do you have to be merry Cratchit? You're poor enough.

SCROOGE tosses the present aside – **BOB** *can't believe it.*

BOB *(finally snaps)* And what reason do you have to be grumpy? – You're rich enough.

BOB *slaps his hand over his mouth – he can't believe he's finally done it.*

SCROOGE *shoots up.*

SCROOGE Bah! Humbug! What else can I be with a world filled with fools such as you? Merry Christmas! Out upon Merry Christmas. What's Christmas but a time for spending money you haven't got? Keep your Merry Christmas in your own way Cratchit and let me keep it in mine.

BOB *composes himself and really wants to know the answer to the following question. He might as well, he's past the point of no return:*

Why are you so afraid of life?

SCROOGE's *anger is slow to rise but when it comes –.*

SCROOGE That's it! Out – you can have tomorrow off and the next day and the day after that.

BOB You're...

SCROOGE I'm teaching you a valuable lesson Cratchit – that there's no such thing as a job for life any more. Clerks are ten a penny.

BOB You can't sack me – it's Christmas Eve.

SCROOGE We have no formal contract. Now leave me alone.

*   **BOB** *knows it's useless to argue further.*

*   **SCROOGE** *holds out* **BOB***'s gift.*

And you can take this with you.

*   **SCROOGE** *throws the present on the floor.*

*   **BOB** *picks up the present, thinks about taking it but lays it on* **SCROOGE***'s desk.*

BOB May you get the Christmas you deserve, sir.

*   **BOB** *leaves.*

SCROOGE Bah! Humbug!

*   *As* **BOB** *goes down into the street...* **SCROOGE** *takes his candle and goes up to his bed (which is above the shop). He takes* **TINY TIM***'s present with him.*

Maybe I'll put this on the fire. Christmas. Bah! Humbug!

*   *As he gets changed into his bed clothes...*

BOB I don't know what to do – sacked on Christmas Eve. Should I tell Tiny Tim I've been sacked? *(He asks audience members).* What you reckon, do you think I should tell Tiny Tim? It'll ruin Christmas.

*   **BOB** *comes to the conclusion:*

Yes, you're right – I shouldn't lie to Tiny Tim. I'll tell him the truth. On Boxing Day.

*   **SCROOGE** *settles down in bed.*

SCROOGE I don't need Bob Cratchit. I'm the reason I'm rich, hard graft has got me to where I am, and being sensible and responsible and... stopping work for a whole day? Humbug!

The candle goes out.

SCROOGE *relights it. He feels the cold.*

Think I'm getting a chill.

The candle goes out again.

The wardrobe door opens on its own. He closes it.

He lights the candle.

Just a draught. Maybe I should eat something before sleep.

He gets a lump of cheese and a pickled onion from under his pillow, blows off any hair and dust and starts to eat.

The candle goes out again.

The place seems colder, darker.

The wardrobe door opens again.

As **SCROOGE** *approaches the door to the wardrobe...*

A noise? The sound of a bell? No, it's duller than that.

Humbug.

Another noise. A rattling. Of chains.

Hello? Who's there?

SCROOGE *picks up a poker – in order to defend himself? He closes the wardrobe door.*

The sound starts to increase – **SCROOGE** *can't work out where it's coming from. The sound grows – it's a clanking, mixed with a slow thud and throbbing, as if someone is dragging a heavy chest up some stairs. Underneath* *is a sort of music that is filled with dread. The lights change – a strangeness (more blue than yellow?), the music builds and builds and builds...*

Then it stops. Quiet.

Then the lights go crazy, the curtains blow, the wind howls, the wardrobe door is flung open. We don't see **MARLEY** *– but he's there.*

MARLEY Ebenezer Scrooge.

SCROOGE *wheels around, still holding the poker.*

Something swirls around the room. It gives **SCROOGE** *a fright, he drops the poker on his foot. It shifts and moves – and the sound of the dragging chains is everywhere.*

SCROOGE Who are you?

MARLEY Ask me who I was.

SCROOGE Is this some sort of parlour game?

MARLEY In life, I was your partner Jacob Marley.

SCROOGE Bah, Hum...humbug!

MARLEY You don't believe me?

SCROOGE Why should I?

MARLEY You don't trust your senses?

SCROOGE A little thing can affect your senses. A slight disorder of the stomach makes them cheat – you might be an undigested piece of beef. There's more gravy than grave to you.

MARLEY Scrooge, you look even Scroogier than when I was alive.

SCROOGE What does "Scroogier" mean?

MARLEY You'll find out. For the past seven years I've been doomed to wander through the world /

SCROOGE You're been travelling for seven years and you've only just got to Mold? – you must have used Transport for Wales.

MARLEY I, Jacob Marley, made my chains, link by link – forged by our greed

SCROOGE Our /?

MARLEY and now I cannot rest, no rest Ebenezer, no peace, burdened by the incessant torture of remorse.

SCROOGE Are your chains heavy?

MARLEY Is a frog's bum water-tight?

SCROOGE You can't be Marley – he'd never make a joke.

MARLEY I've gained one thing since death.

SCROOGE Weight?

MARLEY A sense of humour.

SCROOGE I hate laughter almost as much as I hate Christmas.

MARLEY Do you want to know the length of chain that you drag with you?

SCROOGE I've no chain /

MARLEY You have. Seven years ago your chains were as full and heavy as mine. You've laboured on them since. You just can't see them yet...

SCROOGE Can't I pay someone else to hold them?

MARLEY The man without money is poor; the man with only money is poorer still. My dreadful fate will be your fate Ebenezer, no rest, no peace.

SCROOGE The lack of money is the root of all evil.

MARLEY Tonight, you will be haunted by three spirits. The first will appear to you at midnight. The second at /

SCROOGE Fine, let them haunt me. But can't I meet them all at once and get it over with? I'm usually tucked up in bed by ten.

MARLEY *lets out a ghostly howl. It scares* SCROOGE.

MARLEY Without their help you are doomed to my fate.

SCROOGE *doesn't like the sound of that.*

SCROOGE So without the help of these ghosts I'm doomed to wander the earth carrying heavy chains?

MARLEY That's the gist of it.

SCROOGE How are these ghosts going to help me?

MARLEY, *laughing, starts to move away, his chains clanking.*

MARLEY Your future and past awaits you, Ebenezer.

MARLEY *floats away, his chains trailing behind him.*

SCROOGE Hey, where are you going? What did you mean when you said...? There's a lot of detail you should be filling in about how I can avoid your fate. Marley – I insist you get back here. Marley?

MARLEY Follow me everyone, come on boys and girls, that's right come on, this way, don't worry, Scrooge can't see you. I need your help. This way...hurry up or you won't get back for bedtime...this way, I'm out of here...follow the light...

SCROOGE – *and the audience – follow* MARLEY, *his sounds and a light...*

We are now in a new space – it's a dream-like place where everything is possible. SCROOGE'*s bed is in the centre.*

SCROOGE *settles down in bed but keeps on waking up – with the noise from the audience. He doesn't acknowledge them but knows something strange is going on.*

SCROOGE How very strange. Aaah, it's nothing – I'm in my bedroom even though it looks a bit...odd. I'm probably having a dream. I knew I shouldn't have had that pickled onion. Time to sleep.

Then, when everyone is settled in the space, he starts to fall asleep...

It's just a dream. Maybe a dream within a dream. Or a...

He falls asleep. A noise. He shoots up. There's nothing there.

He settles again. And sleeps. The clock strikes midnight. Up SCROOGE *shoots. He checks his watch.*

It's past midnight. Nothing! I knew it. Stupid. Pickled. Onions.

He goes back to sleep. He snores.

The door to the wardrobe opens.

The **GHOST OF CHRISTMAS PAST** *enters. It has characteristics of* **MRS ROBERTS** *who we met in the first scene. It hands out bells to audience members and keeps one for itself. The* **GHOST** *tells everyone to shhhhh as it creeps up on* **SCROOGE** *– then clangs the bell in* **SCROOGE**'s *ear (encouraging everyone to ring their bell).*

SCROOGE *shoots out of bed – the* **GHOST** *chases him around with the bell, laughing.* **SCROOGE** *is freaking out. The* **GHOST** *quietens the audience –* **SCROOGE** *takes refuge under his blanket, eventually poking his head out.*

Are you the spirit that Jacob Marley told me about?

GHOST OF CHRISTMAS PAST Take a wild guess.

SCROOGE What business do you have?

GHOST OF CHRISTMAS PAST Your welfare.

SCROOGE Thanks – but a good night's sleep might have served me better.

GHOST OF CHRISTMAS PAST Take heed Ebenezer.

SCROOGE Are there many like you? Spirits?

GHOST OF CHRISTMAS PAST There are many – some, like me, of the past, some of the present, and *(indicating the audience)* many of the future – can you see them yet?

SCROOGE I can't see / anything.

GHOST OF CHRISTMAS PAST Take my hand.

SCROOGE I'm not holding hands.

GHOST OF CHRISTMAS PAST What are you, four-years-old? Stand up and hold my hand.

He is compelled to. And the space changes. We rush into the past – the years whizz by **SCROOGE** *and the* **GHOST**.

The sound of laughter and fun.

But that fades to leave a little boy on stage.

Know where we are?

SCROOGE No, I... Can he see us?

GHOST OF CHRISTMAS PAST Not unless I choose so – this is a shadow of what has been.

SCROOGE We're in the past. My old school, I see it now...

The small boy plays with some toys.

That one's got no friends.

GHOST OF CHRISTMAS PAST Recognise him?

They get closer.

SCROOGE Oh, it's... How many hours I played with these toys. Alone.

New characters appear – a princess and a pirate and a genie and...

It's dear old Ali Baba! And Poll the Parrot!

YOUNG SCROOGE And the sultan's groom was turned upside down by the genie – he's on his head.

SCROOGE He deserves to be on his head!

The boy plays.

Poor boy.

The **SCHOOLMASTER** *approaches.*

SCHOOLMASTER Ebenezer?

SCROOGE AND YOUNG SCROOGE Yes?

SCHOOLMASTER Your father has sent you a card, isn't that kind?

The boy tries his best to ignore his teacher.

Shall I read it?

The boy continues to play – but is aware of everything the **SCHOOLMASTER** *is saying.*

He says next Christmas you can visit him and he'll have a home for you both again.

YOUNG SCROOGE He said that last Christmas. Where is he?

SCHOOLMASTER He's /

SCROOGE *(to himself)* In the workhouse.

SCHOOLMASTER He's had to go away for a while – on important business *(I think he's working for the government)* – but the money he saves on accommodation pays for your education, here, you understand?

YOUNG SCROOGE But I want to see him, spend Christmas with him.

SCHOOLMASTER It's best you don't visit him, just now. As I say, he's...away. Good boy.

The **SCHOOLMASTER** *leaves.*

YOUNG SCROOGE I hate father.

SCROOGE No.

YOUNG SCROOGE I hate him, I hate him, I hate him.

YOUNG SCROOGE *recedes into the mists of the past.*

SCROOGE I think I should return to my bed.

GHOST OF CHRISTMAS PAST There is more you need to see. We travel on.

The world is again changed – it's lighter, merrier. We are in a draper shop.

FEZZIWIG *enters. He is followed by his workers and neighbours.*

SCROOGE Is that...? It's Fezziwig! Dear old Fezziwig alive again. My first boss.

FEZZIWIG Friends, neighbours, colleagues, it's Christmas Eve, shut up the shop and let's celebrate!

He instructs everyone in decorating the place for Christmas, it's jolly chaos. Food, drink, music.

Merry Christmas everyone!

A dance starts – of which, **FEZZIWIG** *is at the centre. What he lacks in skill he makes up for in enthusiasm.*

When he's puffed out, he stops.

Ha! Wonderful – there's nothing like the feeling of being perfectly plumb tuckered out, is there?

He faces his apprentice, **DICK**.

You've worked hard this year Dick – here, have a chicken.

Out of his suit he pulls a chicken.

DICK Thank you Mr Fezziwig. Merry Christmas!

GHOST OF CHRISTMAS PAST How a small matter can make people so full of gratitude.

SCROOGE Small? No...it wasn't about the money with Fezziwig – he had the power to make us happy in his deeds, to make work a pleasure or a toil. And he made it happy.

GHOST OF CHRISTMAS PAST Are you looking for someone Ebenezer?

SCROOGE No, I, no one.

FEZZIWIG Mrs Saunders! We might be business rivals but I have something for you too /

MRS SAUNDERS I don't want a / chicken.

FEZZIWIG Have a chicken!

He gets out a chicken and **MRS SAUNDERS** *reluctantly takes it.*

And now to my most wonderful apprentice. Ebenezer.

He faces **SCROOGE** *– who looks to the* **GHOST** *for help.*

SCROOGE I thought you said they couldn't see us?

GHOST OF CHRISTMAS PAST I said if I choose so, and I choose.

FEZZIWIG *shakes* **SCROOGE**'s *hand.*

FEZZIWIG Merry Christmas Ebenezer. Guess what I've got for you?

SCROOGE Uh, is it a chicken?

FEZZIWIG Don't be silly.

Theatrically, he pulls out a fountain pen.

It's a pen with its own ink reservoir – what do you think about that?

SCROOGE It's...delightful. Thank you.

FEZZIWIG Now then, dear everyone, I have some announcements to make. Mrs Saunders here:

MRS SAUNDERS *takes a bow – no one likes her.*

Has offered to buy this place.

Before **MRS SAUNDERS** *can say anything:*

It's a fair offer and Mrs Saunders said to me just the other day /

MRS SAUNDERS It'll make a cracking little factory Fezziwig. The days of small shops like this are over – big business is the way to go.

FEZZIWIG So I have to tell you this will be my last year in business.

MRS SAUNDERS *is delighted.*

There are "no's" and gasps from his workers.

I'm hanging up my apron and scissors.

More "no's" etc.

I'm handing all my shares in the business to /

MRS SAUNDERS *is about to step forward when* **BELLE** *appears in the doorway. She has a drink in her hand.*

SCROOGE Belle.

FEZZIWIG My Isabel.

MRS SAUNDERS What!

FEZZIWIG And that's not all – more big news – Mrs Saunders tells me her son, Tarquin, would like to ask for my daughter's hand in marriage.

MRS SAUNDERS She'll not find a better match in Mold. He's a proper catch, Fezziwig, and no mistake.

FEZZIWIG I think she has your answer, Mrs Saunders.

BELLE You and your stinky son can bog off. I'll find my own husband, thank you very much.

MRS SAUNDERS What!? She /

BELLE *She* is now in control of this store and if *she* asks her employees to throw someone out they'll do it.

FEZZIWIG Now, now Belle, play nice. Is that your third gin?

BELLE This is 1825 father, not 1725 – young women are allowed to enjoy themselves.

MRS SAUNDERS No one dares lay a hand on me.

SCROOGE I'll do it. I'll happily throw you out.

A moment between SCROOGE *and* BELLE.

BELLE *finds this wonderful.*

MRS SAUNDERS Outrageous!

FEZZIWIG It is. Of course. Outrageous. But isn't it brilliant? Let's celebrate. To Belle and to Christmas.

Everyone, except MRS SAUNDERS, *toasts "to Belle and to Christmas".*

MRS SAUNDERS *slopes off.* BELLE *and* SCROOGE *only have eyes for each other across the floor – but they don't come together, they are like two planets orbiting the sun.*

The scene slows – but the world rushes by. Everyone drifts away, apart from BELLE, SCROOGE, FEZZIWIG *and the on-looking* GHOST.

FEZZIWIG *is taking down the decorations.*

BELLE *is making a list.*

BELLE We're not making a profit.

SCROOGE Reduce your outgoings.

BELLE Sack staff?

SCROOGE Maybe make them work a little longer for a little less pay.

BELLE Since you started that business with Marley you've become a right...

She can't think of the word.

SCROOGE We could always give you a small loan to tide you / over.

BELLE Neither a borrower nor a lender be. I can work this out, thank you very much.

BELLE *moves off.*

FEZZIWIG So it's going well, this money-lending thing?

SCROOGE Small personal investment funds.

FEZZIWIG Hmmm. You know I was going to offer you a stake in this place – when I handed it to Belle. But I knew there was no need.

SCROOGE Because I have ambitions?

FEZZIWIG Because I knew you'd be part of the family one day.

SCROOGE What, what do you...mean?

FEZZIWIG She's in love with you.

SCROOGE What? Who? Belle? Me? No. No. *(pause)* You think? How can you tell?

FEZZIWIG You're the only man my Isabel asks advice from – including her father.

SCROOGE *is pleased as punch. He does a little dance.*

SCROOGE I'm in love!

Music strikes up and **BELLE** *and* **SCROOGE** *dance a dance of love.*

Time speeds forward again, Christmases come and go, they get jumbled up together.

And the music slows...

(as they dance) Spirit, no more – I know how this ends.

GHOST OF CHRISTMAS PAST One last shadow...

BELLE *pulls away from him.*

BELLE I won't do it Ben.

SCROOGE If only I could really go back to this time.

BELLE I'd rather burn the store down than sell to Mrs Saunders. And anyway, no one will ever lend her the money to buy this place – everyone had too much respect for my father /

SCROOGE *has to turn away from her gaze.*

Of course. You! You can't resist a coin, can you?

SCROOGE If you don't sell, you'll be poor.

BELLE And what? You won't marry without a dowry?

SCROOGE I'll marry you today – let's run up to St Mary's, find a clergyman and I'll marry you.

BELLE No, you won't.

SCROOGE I only want the best for you.

BELLE You're willing to work with Mrs Saunders against me because you want "the best" for me? When you started this business with Marley you remember what you said? "We're going to lend money to people who need it the most". You've changed Ebenezer.

SCROOGE No, it's still me.

BELLE I used to look in your eyes and I'd see defiance.

SCROOGE And now?

BELLE Why are you so afraid of life?

SCROOGE Come on Belle, we're essentially arguing over money. I'll have plenty in a few years' time to keep up / both.

BELLE You honestly believe this is about money?

SCROOGE I'm wiser about business now, sure, but I've always been the same with you, haven't I?

BELLE Maybe we've outgrown each other.

SCROOGE But I love you Belle.

BELLE And I *would* have loved you for ever.

The music is still playing.

SCROOGE *stands, in position to dance.*

But it's not for BELLE, *she leaves him hanging, she goes.*

SCROOGE No, Belle? Don't...please.

He realises where he is – in bed.

He also realises he's crying. Silly, really, he thinks. Come on SCROOGE *– this isn't like you.*

I was just a boy, a boy who buried his father in a workhouse grave, a boy who could see how easy it would be to slip into... that dark place. You had no idea the misery that poverty brings. I was just a boy, Belle.

He gets up and checks the bedroom, looking for the GHOST. *Nothing in the wardrobe. When he's satisfied there is no one there:*

You're a sentimental old fool Ebenezer Scrooge, letting your imagination run away with you. I've been sleeping and all of this is just a /

A bell. Then more. They are deeper than anything we have heard so far. They transform into a laugh. SCROOGE *gets out of bed, lights a candle and the door to the wardrobe opens. Before him appears the* GHOST OF

CHRISTMAS PRESENT. *It has characteristics of* **MS AUBIN** *who he met in the first scene. With her comes thousands of bubbles.*

You must be another of Marley's friends?

GHOST OF CHRISTMAS PRESENT You don't recognise me, mon cheri?

SCROOGE Should I?

GHOST OF CHRISTMAS PRESENT I am the Ghost of Christmas Present and I spread the spirit of Christmas.

SCROOGE Seasonal worker?

GHOST OF CHRISTMAS PRESENT I'm here to remove some misery from the planet.

SCROOGE You've got your work cut out.

GHOST OF CHRISTMAS PRESENT Ha! You're uglier than I imagined, but funnier. You're on a journey this night.

SCROOGE I'm a reluctant traveller – I get carriage sick.

GHOST OF CHRISTMAS PRESENT Touch my robe, funny man.

SCROOGE Really?

He relents – and the space is again bustling with people preparing for the Christmas church show. **MRS ROBERTS** *is with* **TINY TIM** *who is leaning on his crutch at the side of the action. She shushes the organised chaos and pushes* **TINY TIM** *forward.*

MRS ROBERTS Come on now everyone, Tim has been practising a new song for his dad. Who taught you this one?

TINY TIM *(audience member)* She did.

MRS ROBERTS I hope this isn't as mucky as the last one. Right, you ready to sing?

TINY TIM I'm not sure.

MRS ROBERTS Course you are. What can go wrong – you're with friends... and Mrs Fogarty? Tim told me he's so impressed with your cakes he's going to sing a little song about one. Isn't that wonderful!

TINY TIM *prepares himself.*

Ready? Tim is going to sing...

TINY TIM *(announcing)* "Mrs Fogarty's Cake".

MRS ROBERTS *(to audience member)* How sweet.

TINY TIM *(singing)*
AS I SAT IN MY WINDOW LAST EVENING
THE LETTERMAN BROUGHT IT TO ME
A LITTLE GILT-EDGED INVITATION SAYING
"TINY TIM, COME OVER TO TEA"
I KNEW THE FOGARTIES SENT IT
SO I WENT JUST FOR OLD FRIENDSHIP'S SAKE
THE FIRST THING THEY GAVE ME TO TACKLE
WAS A SLICE OF MRS FOGARTY'S CAKE.

MRS ROBERTS *is enjoying this one...making a point of raising her eyes to* **MRS FOGARTY** *who she respects and a thumbs up to the audience member.*

THERE WERE PLUMS AND PRUNES AND CHERRIES
THERE WERE CITRONS AND RAISINS AND CINNAMON, TOO
THERE WAS NUTMEG AND CLOVES AND BERRIES
AND A CRUST THAT WAS NAILED ON WITH GLUE.

MRS ROBERTS *is less sure...*

THERE WERE CARAWAY SEEDS IN ABUNDANCE
SUCH THAT WORK UP A FINE STOMACH ACHE
THAT COULD KILL A MAN TWICE AFTER EATING A SLICE
OF MRS FOGARTY'S CHRISTMAS CAKE

TINY TIM *starts to cough, it's a big effort for him, but is about to launch into another verse when* **MRS ROBERTS** *stops him.*

MRS ROBERTS I'm so sorry Mrs Fogarty. *(to audience member)* I really can't trust anyone.

MRS FOGARTY *storms off.*

Why did you sing that?

TINY TIM It's true – her cakes are like rocks!

MRS ROBERTS Is your chest bad? Look, maybe you should give up on singing a song for your dad.

TINY TIM I'm going to do it Mrs Roberts – if it kills me.

MRS ROBERTS *fears it might.*

MRS ROBERTS I'm just saying, if you're not well...

TINY TIM, *quietly, starts to cry.*

Hey, hey, hey, no need for that. It's almost Christmas Day. We'll work something out. Come on. Hey, everyone, why don't we sing a song to cheer up Tiny Tim?

The cast sing a song to cheer up **TINY TIM** *– which they encourage the audience to join in with – it's fun but eventually breaks down with plenty of laughter.*

GHOST OF CHRISTMAS PRESENT Why don't you like people?

SCROOGE Why should I like people? They don't like me.

GHOST OF CHRISTMAS PRESENT I've never heard such a whinge-bag as you Scrooge. It's all "moi, moi, moi" with you isn't it? You have to learn to live a little, you funny little man. You don't need cash to have a good time.

SCROOGE But it certainly helps.

GHOST OF CHRISTMAS PRESENT There's joy in picking your nose when you're told not to, patting a dog on the head, painting, drawing, reading your favourite story /

SCROOGE Getting a good night's sleep /

GHOST OF CHRISTMAS PRESENT Volunteering for a charity, helping a stranger, hugging, laughing, singing, dancing /

The Christmas show bursts again into singing and dancing – **SCROOGE** *is pulled into it and, despite his better judgement, gets into it. Santa Claus comes on and screams "It's Chriiiiistmaaaas" (very Noddy Holder) – and everyone is delighted, "Merry Christmas" all around, including in the audience.*

SCROOGE *is now separate from this – he is an onlooker again with the* **GHOST**.

The Christmas celebrations peter out and the crowd parts to reveal a more intimate scene – The **CRATCHIT**s' *single room home.*

BOB CRATCHIT *and* **TINY TIM** *have just finished dinner.*

BOB How was that?

TINY TIM I'm as full as an egg.

BOB It was a great goose, wasn't it?

TINY TIM Thank you Father, I've never seen such a bird.

BOB And, believe it or not, there's pudding and punch.

TINY TIM I'll serve the pudding.

BOB No, maybe it's best /

TINY TIM I want to Dad.

BOB *relents –.*

BOB Okay. I'll serve the punch.

BOB *keeps an eye on* **TINY TIM** *(without* **TINY TIM** *seeing him) as he pours two drinks and* **TINY TIM** *goes to the oven – on his crutch.*

Mind that's hot.

TINY TIM Duh. I'm sick, not stupid.

TINY TIM *starts to cough.*

BOB We'll get you to Doctor Willis first thing Boxing Day – get everything sorted out.

TINY TIM Won't you be at work?

BOB Uh, yes, Mr Scrooge said I can have the day off – so we can spend it together.

TINY TIM Good old Mr Scrooge.

BOB Indeed.

> **TINY TIM** *manages to get the small pudding out of the oven – it's all* **BOB** *can do to stop himself from helping.*

> **TINY TIM** *is unsteady as he carries it back to the table, almost falling. He manages it.*

Good boy. What a feast.

SCROOGE It seems a meagre one.

GHOST OF CHRISTMAS PRESENT But a happy one.

SCROOGE Can they see us?

GHOST OF CHRISTMAS PRESENT No.

SCROOGE Hmmm, the last ghost said that. *(beat)* He'll be okay, though, won't he? The boy?

THE GHOST OF CHRISTMAS PRESENT If he is going to die, he'd better get on with it – and decrease the surplus population.

A moment for **SCROOGE.**

SCROOGE I haven't given Cratchit a raise in six years.

GHOST OF CHRISTMAS PRESENT Too late to give him one now, cheri.

BOB What would you like for Christmas my boy?

TINY TIM Nothing that costs nothing.

BOB Some fresh air?

TINY TIM I'd like for it to snow.

BOB Ha! Wouldn't that be something. I can't arrange that but...

> **BOB** *gets out a present from under the table.*

Merry Christmas Tiny Tim.

TINY TIM What is it?

BOB Open it and find out.

> **TINY TIM** *opens the box and finds a tangerine.*

It's to go with your pudding.

> **TINY TIM** *gives his dad a hug.*

TINY TIM Thank you Dad, it's so...orange! What is it?

BOB Something new – a tangerine.

TINY TIM I might save half for later.

BOB Go wild – eat it all, it's Christmas Day. Now, let's tuck in.

> **TIM** *breaks the tangerine in two and offers half to his dad.*

No, no.

TINY TIM Please.

BOB Just a segment then.

TINY TIM Did Mr Scrooge like my present?

BOB Uh, yes.

> **SCROOGE** *feels in his pocket and gets out the small box* **BOB** *gave him.*

SCROOGE It's good for a boy to spend some time with his dad.

GHOST OF CHRISTMAS PRESENT Time is precious.

SCROOGE There is a...warmth here.

GHOST OF CHRISTMAS PRESENT You recognise it?

SCROOGE I can see it. Yes I can...

> **SCROOGE** *gets drawn closer to the scene while the* **GHOST** *drifts away...*

TINY TIM Did he like it? My present?

BOB Um, oh, yeah, he loved it – couldn't stop talking about it.

TINY TIM Good – took me ages to make it.

> **TINY TIM** *raises his glass.*

To the founder of this feast, Mr Scrooge.

BOB Uh /

TINY TIM What? Did you want to say that?

BOB Well, I do usually say that, yes, but maybe this will be a year of changes for us.

TINY TIM And I bet they'll all be good ones.

BOB Yes, I'm sure they will.

> *They clink glasses and drink.*

I love you.

TINY TIM Don't be so soppy.

BOB Don't be so cheeky.

TINY TIM Do you like Mr Scrooge?

BOB I won't speak ill of anyone on Christmas Day.

TINY TIM Last week you called him an *(remembering)* odious, stingy and unfeeling old grump.

BOB Ah, right. Yes, well, that was a bad day at the office. But today is Christmas Day.

> **TINY TIM** *and* **BOB** *raise their glasses.*

TINY TIM God bless us, one and all.

They drink.

I haven't got you a present.

BOB Not even some snow? That's okay, I have all I need right here.

TINY TIM I've got you two presents.

TINY TIM *gets up on his crutch.*

A song – and a dance! While you've been in work I've been rehearsing – I'm going to be in the Christmas show.

BOB Really?

TINY TIM Next year. Mrs Roberts has been helping me choose a song. She's quite a strict woman, isn't she? Keeps on telling me to sing something different.

BOB You'll be on the stage?

TINY TIM Mrs Roberts says I will be one day, if I keep practising.

BOB *knows this is unlikely but...*

But this year, this song is just for you.

TINY TIM *sings a song – it's not a silly parody but a beautiful song:*

WHAT IS A FANTASTIC THING?
A SHINY SOVEREIGN OR A SUIT WITHOUT HOLES IN?
NO.
A FULL TEA CADDY OR A STORY WITH A GREAT FINALE?
HARDLY.

MY FANTASTIC THING IS YOU.
MY FANTASTIC THING IS SITTING ON YOUR SHOULDERS.
IT MAKES ME BOLDER, AND WHEN I'M OLDER WE'LL SHARE
   SO MANY FANTASTIC THINGS.
LIKE DRINKING DOWN THE PUB WHILE EATING LOTS OF
   GRUB. AND PLAYING IN THE SNOW.

ON WE'LL GO, MAKING ANGELS TILL OUR CHEEKS GLOW RED
AND WE'LL NEVER DREAD A SINGLE DAY.

WE'LL ALWAYS BE THAT FANTASTIC THING.

NEVER BE SAD, BECAUSE IT'S JUST ME AND YOU, MY
FANTASTIC DAD.

It ends in a coughing fit, **TINY TIM***'s over done it.*

BOB *settles him in his chair.*

BOB Bravo, my wonderful boy.

SCROOGE Ghost? Where are you?

He searches for the **GHOST** *but can't find it – he gets
more desperate.*

Ghost? Is he very ill, the boy? Tiny Tim? Where are you?
Answer me. *(pause)* He's going to be okay? Will Tiny Tim
live? Say he will be spared.

SCROOGE *is drawn back to the* **BOB** / **TINY TIM** *scene:*

TINY TIM *is in* **BOB***'s lap:*

BOB That's it Tim, time for a sleep.

SCROOGE Does anyone love me, Spirit?

He waits for an answer, there is none.

*Then, suddenly, there is a party. The group of people
are waiting for someone to come back into the room...
as* **BELLE** *does she shouts at the open door behind her:*

BELLE Now play quietly in there with your presents' children –
don't make me send your father in.

MRS TOPPER Is that some kind of threat Richard? Do you beat
them?

RICHARD Lord no, it's no threat. The girls hate playing with me, I always mess up their games. It's Isabel they all want to play with.

BELLE Nonsense Richard, you were marvellous at Snapdragon last night.

RICHARD I kept on burning my fingers! The girls found it ridiculous.

BELLE You are ridiculous.

RICHARD Taking of ridicule /

BELLE Were we?

RICHARD You'll never guess who I saw yesterday?

BELLE Is this your new game?

RICHARD Six o'clock on Christmas night and still scratching away at his ledger by the light of a candle.

MRS TOPPER There's only one man in Mold who'd be so unseasonal /

RICHARD That's right – your old friend, Mr Scrooge.

MRS TOPPER I don't think he even believes in Christmas. He has a heart of stone.

BELLE No. He doesn't.

SCROOGE That's right Belle, tell them.

RICHARD Now come on Isabel you've got to admit he is a strange fellow.

BELLE He has a heart. Before Daddy died /

SCROOGE Tell them I'm a good man.

BELLE When I knew him, he had such noble dreams /

SCROOGE The dreams were for us.

MRS TOPPER A lucky escape Isabel.

BELLE No – we just wanted different things in the end.

A moment – **SCROOGE** *wishes he could reach out and touch* **BELLE**.

Now, enough of this – we need less idle chat and more games. Come on, what shall we play?

RICHARD How about...

Everyone gets excited about **RICHARD**'s *suggestion and we play a game – in an ideal world it would involve everyone in the theatre.*

Can we get everyone to join in with a Victorian game of Forfeits? The audience can help with the descriptions of the item chosen by one of the characters?

Then there might be a clapping game that the whole audience takes part in?

Whatever the games **SCROOGE** *gets mightily excited by them (ref: Albert Finney as* **SCROOGE** *in the 1970 film version of* A Christmas Carol*).*

SCROOGE We used to play this at Fezziwig's office party. I was excellent at this.

He joins in even though no one can see him. He loses himself in the games until:

BELLE That's it! Enough. This is getting out of hand.

RICHARD Oh come on, Isabel, one more game.

SCROOGE Yes, one more game Belle.

BELLE No, we have to put the children to bed. Enough of this madness.

SCROOGE Bring the children in – they can play too!

MRS TOPPER When Isabel speaks we all listen.

RICHARD Quite right too.

Everyone says their "goodbye"s and "thank you"s (SCROOGE stands in the line, thanking everyone for a wonderful night). RICHARD shows the last of the guests out. As they leave:

MRS TOPPER All these games have worn me out.

MR TOPPER We should play games more often, not just at Christmas.

MRS TOPPER Shall we get a carriage home?

MR TOPPER Maybe walk, yes? It's not that cold.

MRS TOPPER I think a carriage would be better.

MR TOPPER Yes, dear.

> **BELLE** *is alone.*

SCROOGE Ghost, can you hear me? Make her see me now. Just give me one moment with her...

> **RICHARD** *returns.*

Do it Spirit, make me real in front of her – I know you have the power.

RICHARD Thank you.

BELLE For what? Making fun of you in front of our friends?

RICHARD For our life together.

> **BELLE** *and* **RICHARD** *kiss. It stuns* **SCROOGE.**

SCROOGE *(pleading to the unseen* **GHOST**, *on the verge of tears)* This is too much.

Back in his bedroom, he slumps into an armchair.

This is madness, surely? Some kind of waking dream that...

He feels in his pocket and brings out the present from **TINY TIM.**

He almost seems fearful of opening it but he does. Inside is a simple, paper decoration of a snowflake that TINY TIM *has made. (Maybe same as the ones on the Christmas tree in the High Street?).*

SCROOGE *fixes it to his mantelpiece and stands back. It seems to shine brighter than it should.*

My only Christmas decoration. Thank you Tiny Tim. I wish I could talk to your father now. Feel some of the warmth the two of you have. But what would I do with warmth? Family? Love? Is all that beyond me now? I threw away my chance.

He goes towards the bed.

Come, bring on your worst – I know there's one more ghost to come. Where are you? Huh? Show yourself.

SCROOGE *scours the stage looking for the next* GHOST – *and finds nothing. It takes all the energy out of him.*

Show yourself.

The wardrobe door opens – and the GHOST *emerges. The* GHOST OF CHRISTMAS FUTURE. *It has characteristics of* TINY TIM. *There is a different atmosphere from the other* GHOSTs – *for a moment* SCROOGE *is scared.*

Suddenly the stage is again filled with revellers. We are in the street. It seems like a holiday.

I fear you more than any spectre I have seen. I suspect what you will tell me – that I was despised for the rest of my life, that this town still cowers under the financial empire I built. Show me the worst of it. Are these shadows of what is to come?

You're the Ghost of Christmas Future?

The GHOST *nods.*

The GHOST *waves its arm and...*

MRS ROBERTS What a day. What a wonderful Christmas present – and we have one man to thank...thank you, Mr Scrooge.

BEGGAR Here's to the man of the hour – Ebenezer Scrooge!

SCROOGE Ha, ha, hear that Spirit? They like me. They love me. They sing my name. I've got it – I know what happens; in the future I change. I can change and I do change – I'm the toast of the town. My story has a happy ever after. Where am I? I've always been a modest hero.

MRS ROBERTS I wish I'd been there the day the bailiffs turned up to his door.

BEGGAR I wish I'd been there when they served the bankruptcy notice on him.

SCROOGE Bailiffs? Bankrupt?

MRS ROBERTS Who would have thought it – it was Bob Cratchit who was holding the business together. With Scrooge bankrupt all our debts are wiped away! When he sacked Bob /

BEGGAR The place went to wrack and ruin.

MRS ROBERTS "Humbug, I don't need anyone else. I can manage on my own." Oh, I wish I'd seen him enter the Poorhouse.

BEGGAR What a sight it was. I was there, front row. But he was proud to the last – "Any chance I can have my own room? Will it be ensuite?"

Everyone finds great joy in this.

Now he sits there alone, in a corner of the infirmary, surrounded by the poor he put in there.

MRS ROBERTS I hear he's gone mad, babbles on all day.

BEGGAR They've had to chain him to his bed. He daren't sleep just in case one of the others...

MRS ROBERTS I can't believe we're free from his debt.

BEGGAR Thank you Ebenezer Scrooge. And Merry Christmas.

We hear **SCROOGE**. *It has the same quality of sound we heard from* **MARLEY** ...

SCROOGE About time we had a reckoning – write me a list and add it up. A man should know his worth.

Tuesday it is then, or I send the bailiffs.

Are there no prisons? And the workhouses? The Poorhouse? Still in operation?

I wish to be left alone. Those who are badly off – it's their own fault they're poor. They can go to the workhouse.

I wish to be left alone...

BOB CRATCHIT *appears.*

SCROOGE Bob!

BOB *buys some flowers from a seller:*

BOB Give me the brightest bunch – they're for Tiny Tim.

SCROOGE He lives? That's wonderful news.

The **GHOST** *points.*

And **BOB** *arrives at the grave of* **TINY TIM**. *He lays the flowers down.*

Oh no Spirit, tell me this is not true.

BOB I can't believe it's Christmas Eve again – where does the time go?

SCROOGE He looks older.

BOB Remember when I used to carry you on my shoulders Tim? How you love Christmas, don't you? Remember you sang me that wonderful song, you'd been rehearsing? I wish I... could have given you a better present, ha! I wish I could have made it snow for you before...but, hey, come on, it's

Christmas Eve. No need to be sad. I've got dinner at Mrs Roberts's tomorrow. Merry Christmas, my Tiny Tim.

SCROOGE Oh, no, no, no. This isn't right Spirit. Tiny Tim. I never wanted this.

The **GHOST** *starts to walk away.*

This isn't fair. I *could* have changed. Will anyone mourn the loss of Ebenezer Scrooge? Will no one lay flowers on my grave? Not even Belle?

The **GHOST** *stops.*

The **GHOST** *turns – it points at the audience.*

I will? How? A kind word? Maybe a statue?

Depending on the answers, he gets to ask:

What do you think of when you hear the word "Scrooge"?

This, of course, makes **SCROOGE** *think. It saddens him.*

He asks the audience:

If I had one wish, it wouldn't be to be remembered fondly. I'd go back in time and change myself. Not to save my life, but to save Tiny Tim's.

To the **GHOST OF CHRISTMAS FUTURE***:*

Tell me Spirit that I may yet change these shadows you have shown me, by an altered life? I can change. I will honour Christmas in my heart and keep it all the year. I promise I'll live in the past, the present and the future, if you just give me a chance. Tell me I can sponge away this future and make a fresh one.

The **GHOST** *will not answer him.*

Take me back to Christmas morning and you'll see I can change. Can't you give me a chance?

The GHOST *disappears in a storm of light and bells.*

Then nothing. SCROOGE *is wrapped in his bed sheets.*

Aaargh, it's all dark!

He removes the bed sheet.

Where am I? Is this the future? Poor old Tiny Tim. Ahhh, I see the spirits linger on – keeping me company are you? That's kind of you but there's no need, I'm used to my own company. Could you do me one last favour before you go? Help me to understand about Christmas, tell me why people love it.

SCROOGE *asks the audience what's good about Christmas, what their favourite thing is. He gradually gets into it – how wonderful it can be (a sense of the enthusiasm he had in* BELLE's *parlour games). But, eventually:*

Sounds magical – except I've missed all that.

Then he notices something – he rushes to TINY TIM's *decoration.*

But this is still here – and my cheese and pickle! That means... This isn't the future... This is my bed, these are my bed sheets – it's now! I'm not in the future, I'm in the now. The shadows of the future can be dispelled. I know they can.

He rushes around the room – giddy with excitement.

I don't know what to do. What should I do? I'm as light as a feather, happy as an angel, merry as a schoolboy. Giddy as a drunken man! Merry Christmas to everyone and a Happy New Year to the whole world.

He gets out a calendar.

The 25th of December...

To the audience:

What's today?

He gets back the answer of "Christmas Day".

I haven't missed Christmas – the spirits did it all last night. I've got a brilliant idea. But I need your help.

SCROOGE *then asks the audience where he can buy certain things – like Christmas decorations, mistletoe, a turkey, some of the foodstuffs sold at the start (the audience should say the street we were in...).*

SCROOGE *lashes the kids / audience with praise:*

"What a delightful boy! An intelligent boy."

"What a delightful young girl – you must be very proud."

SCROOGE *also says he needs a painter, maybe a carpenter...*

When all of that is done... (to an audience member – who is helped by an usher).

And you, will you please go and give Bob Cratchit a message? – I want to see him at my office right away!

A moment – he's out of breath with the wonderfulness of it all...then:

Come on everyone, we've got some celebrating to do! This way!

He leads the audience into another space.

It's the same one as the start of the play – the same street – but now it has been imbued with the spirit of Christmas. It's brighter, cheerier, glowing. It's busy. He goes towards his office (the sign of which is covered over) which is now decorated.

Ha! Merry Christmas. Merry Christmas to you. Mrs Roberts! Merry Christmas to you.

MRS ROBERTS I think Mr Scrooge is having a funny turn.

BEGGAR He looks...different.

SCROOGE You know that money you owe me?

MRS ROBERTS How could I forget?

SCROOGE Keep it – in fact, here, have some more. And we've arranged for a carpenter to fix your roof and here, here's the deeds to your house. It's yours!

MRS ROBERTS Whatever the /

SCROOGE And you *(the* **BEGGAR***)* here's some cash – go and spend it on a good time.

BEGGAR I will!

    BOB *and* **TINY TIM** *approach.*

BOB *(weary)* Mr Scrooge, you sent for me /

MR SCROOGE Mr Cratchit! – and Tiny Tim!

BOB Uh, yes sir, say hello, Tim.

TINY TIM Who are you?

BOB Uh, this is Mr / Scrooge.

MR SCROOGE I'm Ebenezer.

    They shake hands.

TINY TIM Pleased to make your acquaintance.

BOB We're just about to put lunch on, so if you don't mind /

MR SCROOGE It's about your position at Marley and Scrooge, Mr Cratchit.

BOB Uh, yeah, can we discuss this later, not in front of the boy, don't want to spoil Christmas Day /

TINY TIM What's going on?

SCROOGE You know you invited me to Christmas lunch?

BOB Really? After you...

TINY TIM Is he coming for lunch?

BOB Um, yeah, suppose we can make the goose stretch.

SCROOGE You're still willing to serve me lunch even though I sacked you?

TINY TIM You've been sacked?! You told me everything was going well.

BOB Come on, it's Christmas Day.

TINY TIM You told me never to lie.

BOB I was going to tell you – tomorrow.

SCROOGE Remarkable. Well, I'm doing Christmas lunch this year.

The turkey arrives in style – it is so large four people have to carry it.

TINY TIM Look at the size of that!

SCROOGE I know, isn't it a beauty? We can stuff it with your goose.

TINY TIM Is that for us?

BOB I'm not sure it'll fit in your oven.

SCROOGE *(disappointed)* Oh, yes, ah, didn't think of that.

BEGGAR You can cook it bit by bit.

SCROOGE Brilliant idea – there's enough for the whole town!

TINY TIM Best Christmas ever. Apart from you getting the sack. This Christmas cannot get any better.

It starts to snow.

It's snowing!

SCROOGE Yes, I believe your dad arranged it.

TINY TIM Did you?

BOB Me and the weather have an understanding.

SCROOGE Now about your position Bob.

BOB You're going to give me my old job back, aren't you, Mr Scrooge? Well, to be honest, I'm not sure I want it – I might go freelance. Unless, you're offering another tuppenny a day...

SCROOGE No, you've worked your last day as a clerk at Marley and Scrooge.

BOB Oh.

SCROOGE But...

> **SCROOGE** *indicates for a cover on the sign above his business to be revealed. It says Scrooge and Cratchit, est. 1843.*

You're to have a full half share in the business Bob.

BOB What?

TINY TIM Bloody Nora.

BOB Language Tiny Tim!

SCROOGE Don't know why I didn't think of it before. In fact, I might take a back seat – I've discovered a fondness for travelling.

BOB No, I /

SCROOGE Bob?

BOB I'm not sure I'm comfortable /

SCROOGE You want it to be Cratchit and Scrooge? – no problem, we'll get it repainted.

BOB No, I'm not sure I'm comfortable being a money lender.

SCROOGE Nor me – dreadful business. We'll be a charitable foundation. That sort-of French lady who visited us gave me the idea – we're going to help anyone in Mold who needs our help. And, a new concept, we'll be non-profit. What do you think about that?

BOB *is a bit stunned.*

TINY TIM Shake on it Dad, you won't get a better offer!

They shake.

SCROOGE Spoken like a true champion Tim. And for you we'll get the finest doctors and the best medicines.

TINY TIM If Dad is your partner in business then that makes you like an uncle.

SCROOGE An uncle? Uncle Scrooge? Imagine that.

BOB Imagine that.

TINY TIM *gives* **SCROOGE** *a hug.*

SCROOGE Ha! Uncle Scrooge – that's the best Christmas present I have ever received. By the way everyone – all your debts are cancelled!

TINY TIM Merry Christmas one and all.

SCROOGE Yes, let's make it the merriest one we can!

Music starts up and the people of Mold have a rare old time.

A rendition of **"WE WISH YOU A MERRY CHRISTMAS"** *(perhaps?) as people greet each other and play in the snow.*

There's a dance – which everyone can join in with.

SCROOGE *surveys the scene, still not able to fully join in.*

But he's pulled into the fun by **TINY TIM** *and has a wonderful time, making up for all the Christmases that he's missed.*

Ends

Lightning Source UK Ltd.
Milton Keynes UK
UKHW021812150120
357016UK00005B/15/P